SNAKES
AROUND THE WORLD

George S. Fichter

SNAKES
AROUND THE WORLD

Illustrated by Frankie Coventry

AN EASY-READ FACT BOOK

FRANKLIN WATTS
NEW YORK | LONDON | TORONTO | SYDNEY | 1980

Library of Congress Cataloging in Publication Data

Fichter, George S.
  Snakes around the world.

  (An Easy-read fact book)
  Includes index.
  SUMMARY: Introduces the physical characteristics
and habits of snakes and describes various species
of these reptiles.
    1. Snakes—Juvenile literature. [1. Snakes]
I. Coventry, Frankie. II. Title.
QL666.06F37   598.1'2   78-9774
ISBN 0-531-02275-7

R. L. 2.9 Spache Revised Formula

A snake does not have legs. It is covered with scales. It feels dry when touched, not moist and slimy. Many kinds of snakes are really beautiful, with bright colors, stripes, and blotches.

Rainbow boa

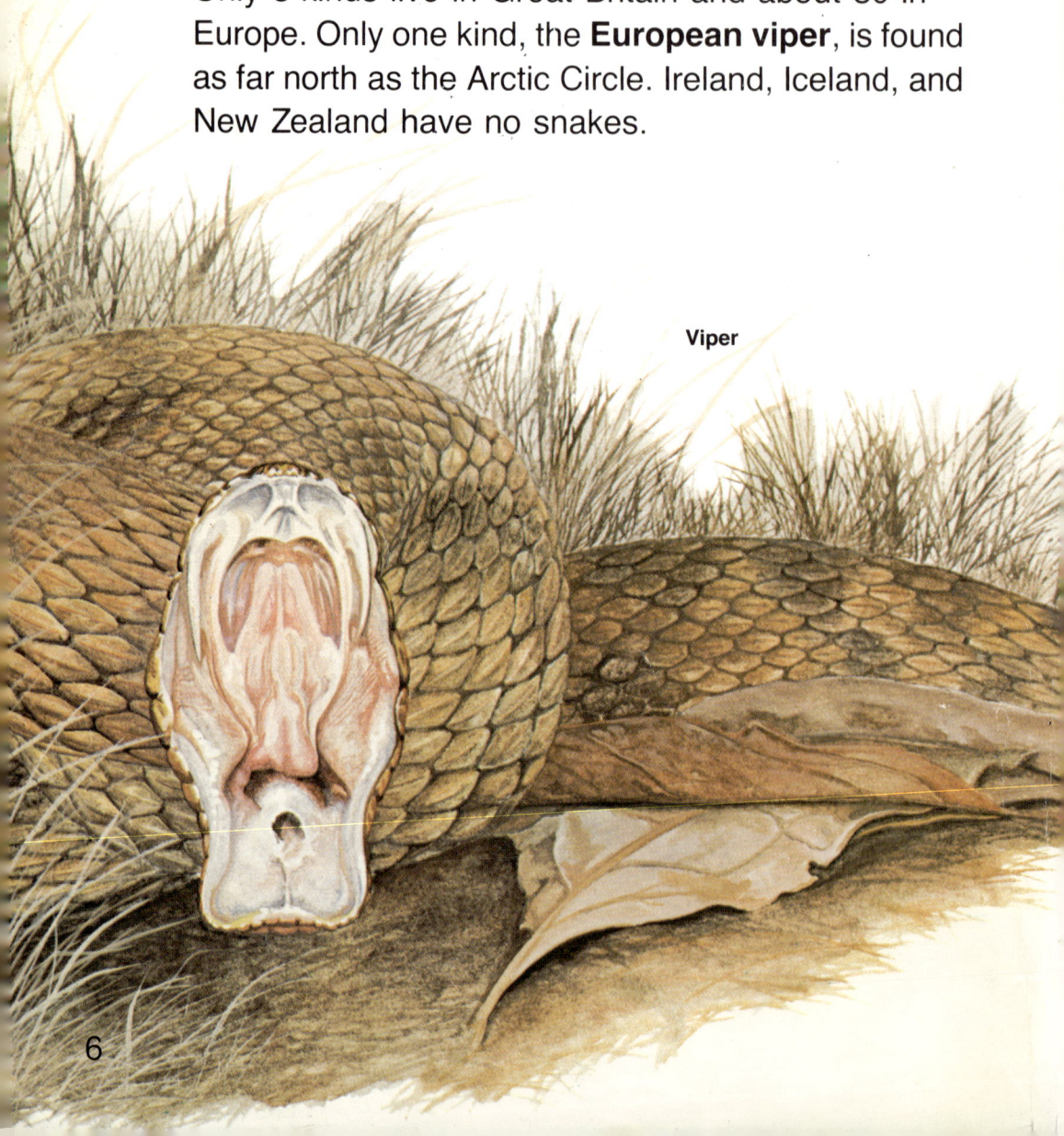

More than 2,500 kinds of snakes live in the world. Most snakes live in warm, wet places. In the United States, there are more than 100 kinds of snakes. Only 3 kinds live in Great Britain and about 30 in Europe. Only one kind, the **European viper**, is found as far north as the Arctic Circle. Ireland, Iceland, and New Zealand have no snakes.

Viper

Snakes are reptiles. Their living relatives are the crocodiles and alligators, lizards, turtles, and the rare tuatara (too-a-TAH-ra) that lives only in New Zealand.

Most snakes are harmless. Many are friends in a way because they eat rats, mice, and other pests.

Boa constrictor

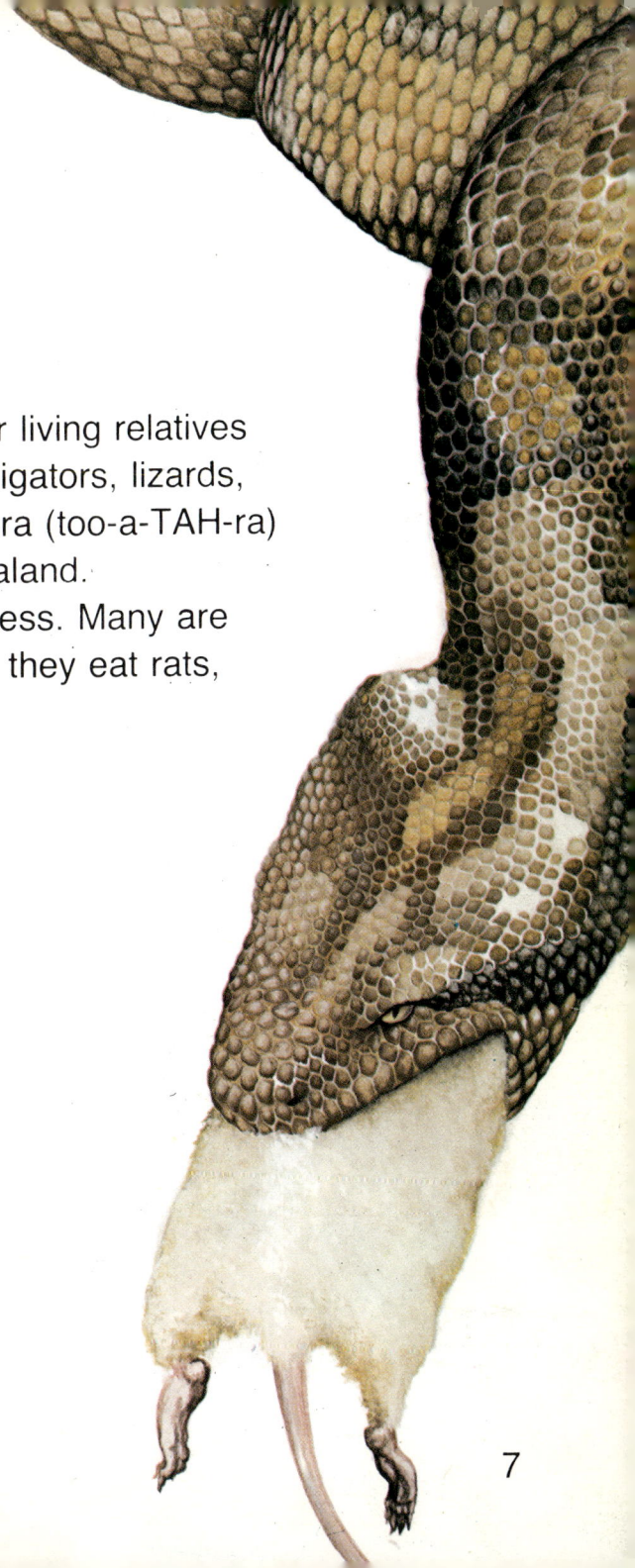

Sea snake

Like other reptiles, snakes breathe air. Even those that live in water must come to the surface from time to time to get a new supply of air.

Snakes are also cold-blooded. Their body temperature is about the same as their surroundings. They are active in warm weather. But they become sluggish as the weather cools. In winter, they crawl into holes or cracks to hibernate.

Fer-de-lance

A snake's back and sides are covered with scales. In some kinds, the scales are smooth. In others, the scales have a ridge, or keel, down the center. The broad, flat belly scales help a snake in crawling. A thin skin covers the scales. And there is a clear cap over each eye.

Russell's viper

Grass snake shedding skin

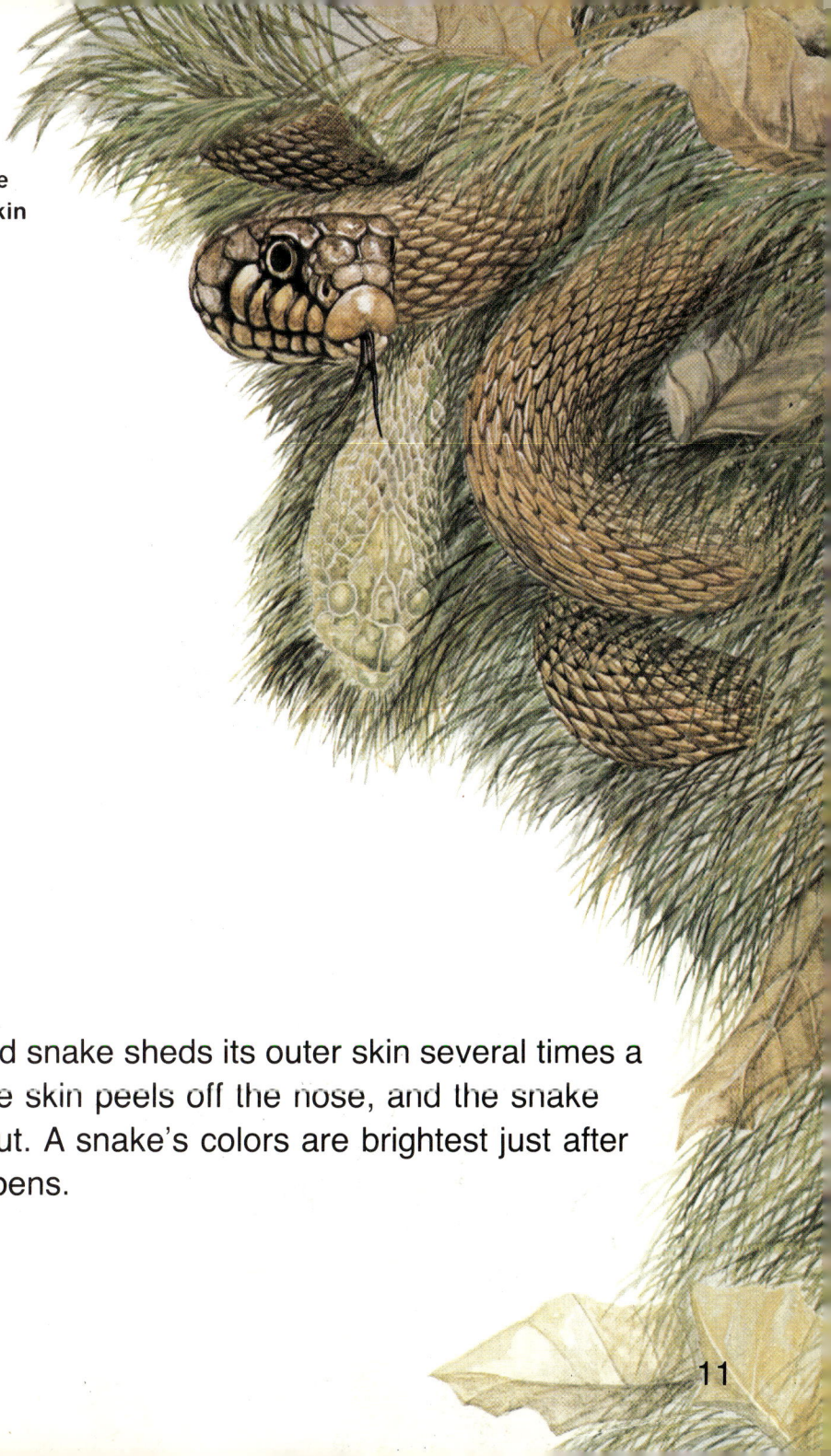

A well-fed snake sheds its outer skin several times a year. The skin peels off the nose, and the snake crawls out. A snake's colors are brightest just after this happens.

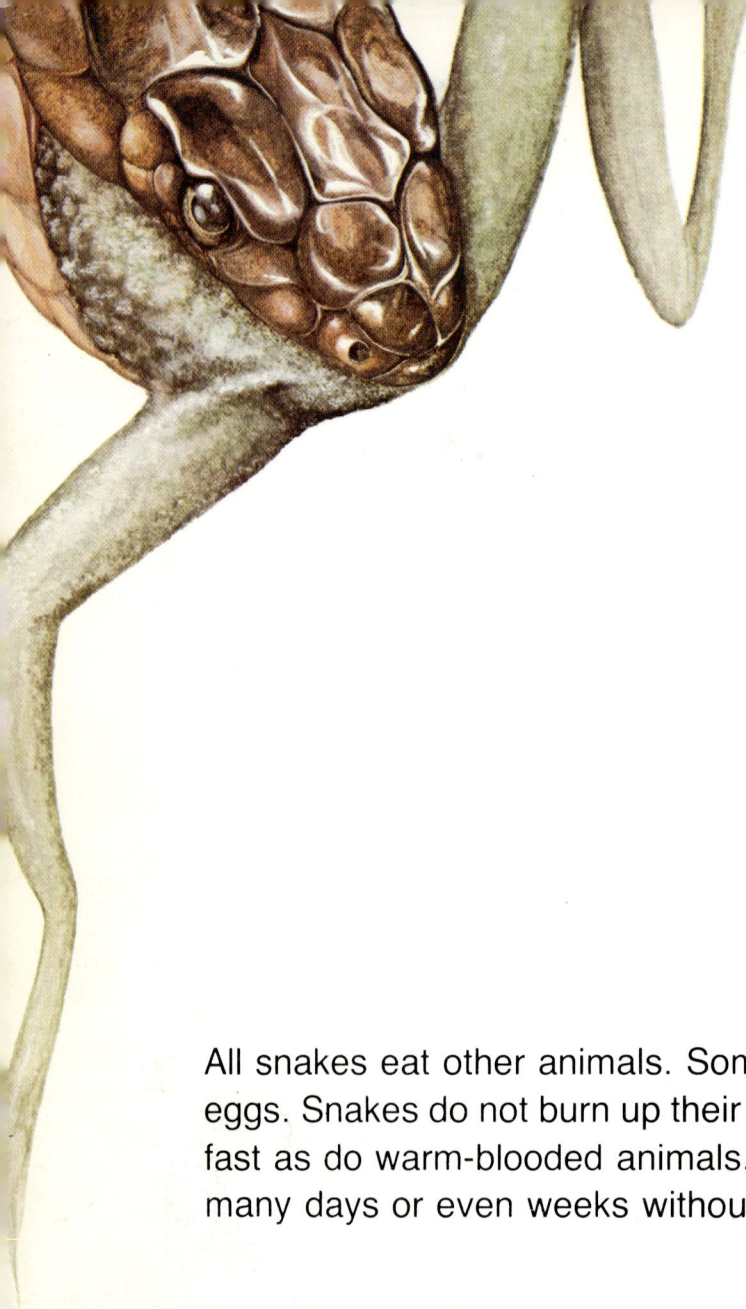

Snake swallowing frog

All snakes eat other animals. Some kinds eat only eggs. Snakes do not burn up their food for energy as fast as do warm-blooded animals. They can go many days or even weeks without eating.

Some snakes put loops of their body over an animal to keep it from fighting back. Then they swallow it alive. **Constrictors** wrap coils of their body around victims. Each time the animal lets out air, the snake tightens its coils. The animal dies quickly by suffocation.

Python eating rat

Poisonous snakes have special teeth called fangs. These are either hollow or have grooves. Poison flows down these fangs into the bite wound. These snakes use their poison for protection as well as for getting food. The poison of some kinds is very powerful. It can kill animals many times the snake's size.

Cobra catching rat

**Tentacled snake
swallowing fish**

A snake swallows its food whole—starting with the head. Its many tiny teeth are curved back, like little hooks. The snake's meal can move only in one direction—into the snake.

A snake can swallow large animals. The right and left halves of the lower jaw are joined in front by a tough band, or ligament. This stretches to let the jaws spread wider. The lower jaws disconnect from the upper jaws to make the mouth still larger.

Egg-eating snake

Swallowing may take an hour or longer.
To breathe when swallowing, a snake sticks
the end of its windpipe out between its
lower jaws. Finally the food is inside
the snake's stomach. There it shows
as a big lump until digested.

Python

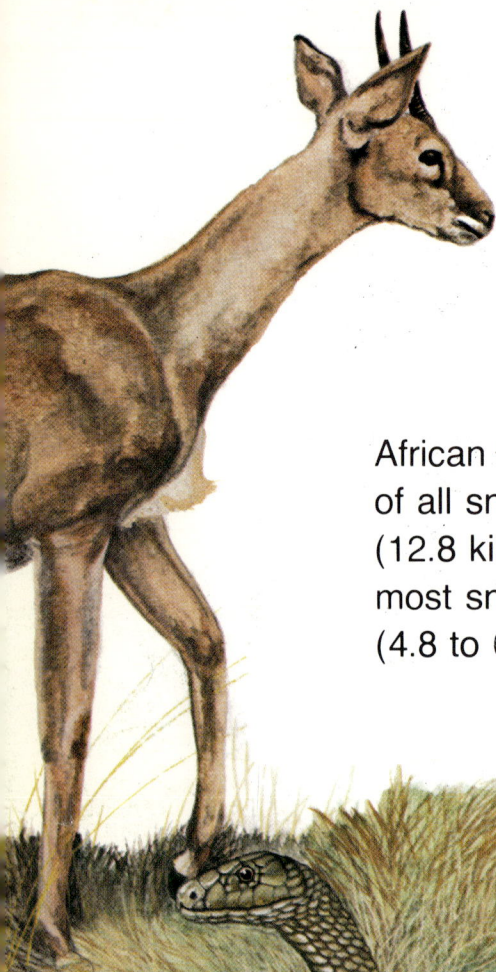

African **black mambas** are the fastest of all snakes. They can go 8 miles (12.8 kilometers) an hour. At top speed, most snakes crawl only 3 to 4 miles (4.8 to 6.4 kilometers) an hour.

Black mamba

To go fast, snakes wriggle their bodies in S-shaped waves. Using only the broad scales on their belly, snakes can crawl slowly in a straight line. Some kinds of desert snakes are "sidewinders." They throw a large loop of their bodies to the side. Then they quickly pull their heads and tails to one side to meet it.

Sidewinder

19

Female python with her eggs

Most female snakes lay eggs. The eggs are round or oblong and white or cream-colored. Their "shell" is tough and like leather.

The female lays her eggs in rotting leaves or wood. The heat from the decay helps to hatch them. Most female snakes do not stay near the eggs.

The baby snake cuts its way out of the egg. It uses a cone-shaped "egg tooth" at the tip of its nose. This "tooth" falls out in a few days. A baby snake must get its own food. It must protect itself from the minute it enters the world.

Young pythons hatching

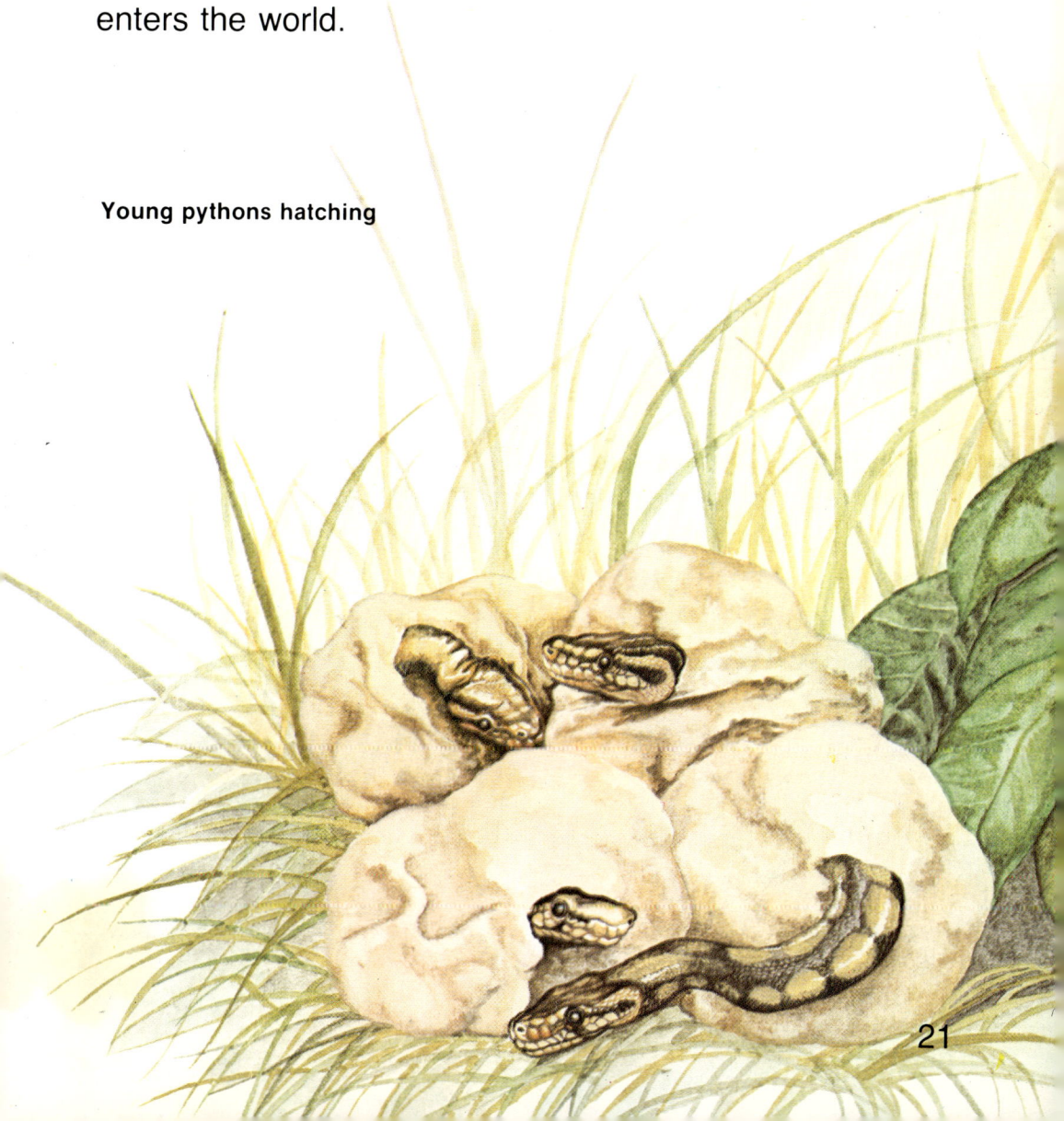

Some kinds of snakes give birth to their young. The female snake's eggs are inside her body until they hatch.

The **common garter snake** may give birth to as many as 70 baby snakes at a time.

Female garter snake and young

Green python

A snake's ears are inside its body. Because of this it cannot hear sounds in the air. It is a snake charmer's swaying body, and not the music of the flute, that holds the snake's attention.

**Viper
showing tongue**

The snake's forked tongue is its most useful sense organ. It is soft and delicate, not a "stinger." The tongue is flicked in and out all the time. The forked tips fit into pits in the roof of the mouth. Here special cells record tastes and smells.

Diagram of skull and part of snake skeleton, showing only one of each pair of ribs

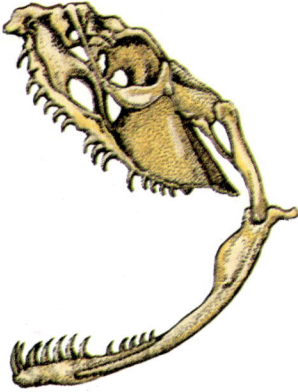

A snake can twist, turn, and kink its body. Its backbone has many separate bones. Some snakes have as many as 300 pairs of ribs. The slim outer tips of the ribs are joined by muscles to the broad scales on the belly.

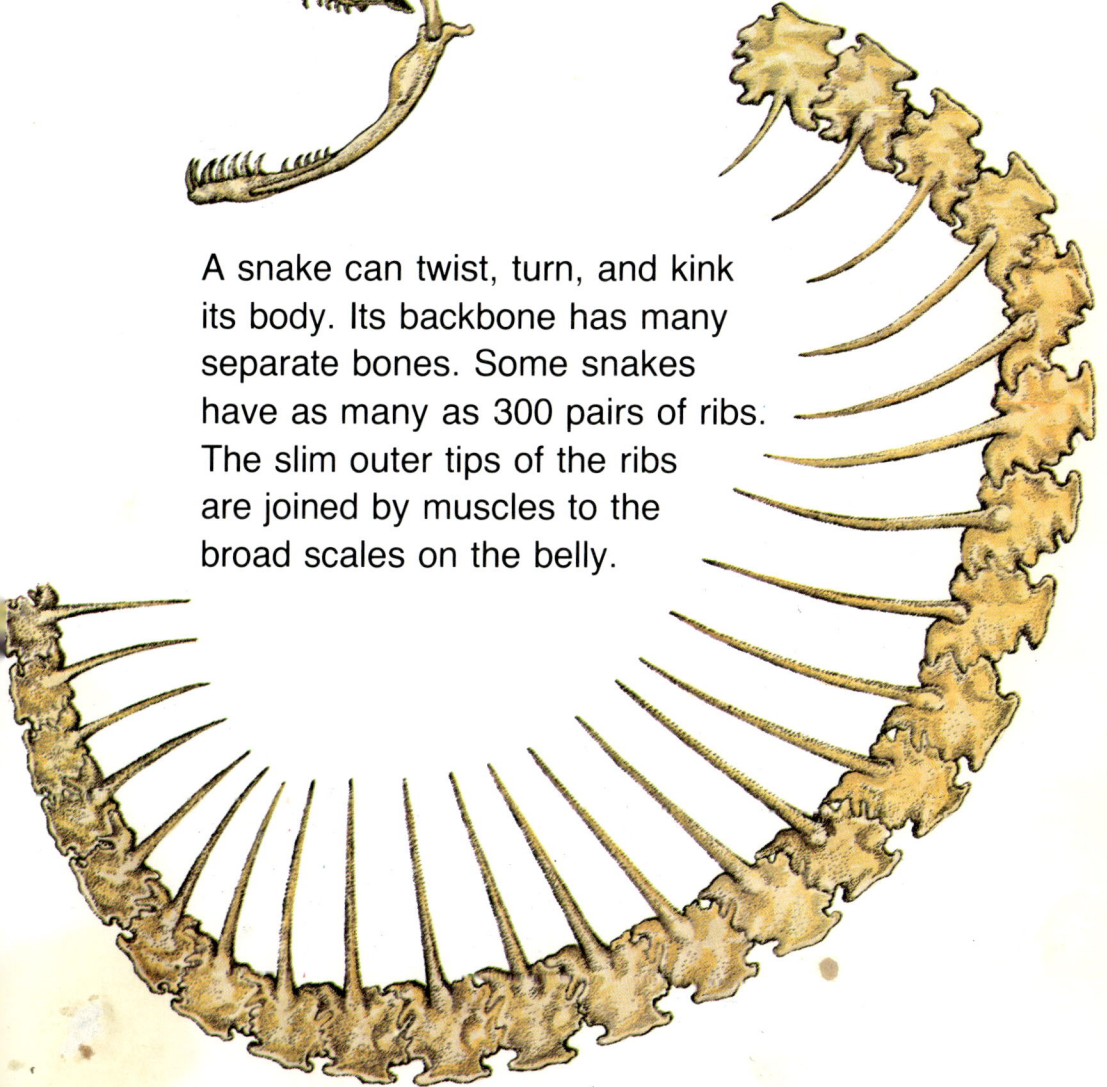

Secretary bird with snake

Snakes have many enemies. Some kinds of snakes, in fact, eat only other snakes.

Hogs are great snake enemies. Sometimes they are put into fields, woods, or brushy places to get rid of rattlesnakes.

African secretary birds eat many snakes.

The Asian mongoose is an enemy of cobras. A mongoose will die if bitten by a cobra. But it dodges the snake's strikes. When the cobra gets tired, the mongoose darts in and bites the snake behind its head.

People are the greatest enemies of snakes. They destroy the places where snakes live. They also kill snakes—even kinds that do not harm people and often help them.

Mongoose and snake

Anaconda

Ball python

Boas and pythons are large snakes that live mostly in very warm places.

Boas can be found in South and Central America. Most famous is the **boa constrictor**. It may be as long as 12 feet (3.6 meters). The **anaconda**, a kind of boa, can be as long as 30 feet (9.1 meters). This heavy-bodied snake lives in or near water.

Pythons of Asia and Africa are primitive snakes with stubs of hind legs inside their bodies. The Asian **reticulated python** can be as long as 33 feet (10 meters). It is the largest of all snakes.

Cobras

The largest of all poisonous snakes is the **king cobra** of southeastern Asia. It may reach a length of 18 feet (5.4 meters). The king cobra feeds on other snakes.

When bothered, a cobra lifts the front of its body off the ground. It spreads its hood. The poison from a bite of one of these giants is enough to kill several people.

Other kinds of cobras live in Asia and Africa. The **Egyptian cobra**, or **asp**, is believed to be the snake that Cleopatra used to kill herself.

The **spitting cobras** of Africa spit their venom. They can make a perfect hit at a distance of eight feet (2.4 meters) or more. They aim for the eyes. The stinging poison can cause blindness.

Spitting cobra

African mamba

African relatives of the cobras are the dangerous
mambas. They are thin and may be 15 feet (4.5
meters) long. Mambas chase and attack people and
animals. Their bites can kill.

The **scarlet snake** is harmless. It is believed that it copies the pattern of the poisonous North American **coral snake** to scare off enemies.

Scarlet snake

Coral snakes are usually shy. They have small fangs. They must chew to get venom into a bite. A small amount of their poison can kill.

South American coral snake

About 50 kinds of **sea snakes** live in the warm waters of the Pacific and Indian oceans. One kind swims through the open ocean to the shores of South and Central America. All sea snakes are poisonous. The venom of some is stronger than a cobra's. But they don't bite often, even if handled.

Sea snake

36

Sea snake

At times, millions of sea snakes swarm at the surface. They are fine swimmers, and some cannot move on land. They have large lungs. They can take in enough air to last for several hours when they dive.

More than 20 kinds of rattlesnakes live in the United States. Largest is the **Eastern diamondback,** sometimes reaching 8 feet (2.4 meters) in length. Smallest is the **pigmy rattlesnake,** rarely more than 1 1/2 feet (.45 meters) long.

Diamondback rattlesnake

Copperhead

A rattlesnake does not always give a warning "rattle" before it strikes.

Each time the snake sheds, often several times a year, another "button" is added to the rattle.

Two poisonous relatives of rattlesnakes in the United States are the **copperhead** and the **cottonmouth**, or **water moccasin**.

Rattlesnakes belong to a group of poisonous snakes called **vipers**. All vipers have long, hinged front fangs. They fold against the roof of the mouth when not in use. These hollow fangs are used like needles to stick in the venom.

Rattlesnake

Vipers showing fangs and tongue

Other dangerous vipers are the **fer-de-lance** (fer-da-LANS) and the **bushmaster** of the American tropics. Another is **Russell's viper** of southeastern Asia. It is said to cause more human deaths than any other snake. The **gaboon viper** of tropical Africa may have fangs 2 inches (5 centimeters) long.

Racer

The thin, fast **racers** are common snakes that do not harm people. Racers are easily excited. They are quick to bite. But they only tear the skin with their sharp, curved teeth.

Another group of harmless snakes is called **rat snakes** because they like to eat rodents. Most of them are either blotched or striped. They tame quickly.

Rat snake

King snake

King snakes eat other snakes. They do not hunt for rattlesnakes, as many believe. But they do not run away when they find them. A king snake may die if a rattlesnake bites it.

Eastern diamondback rattlesnake

The **scarlet king snake** looks much like a coral snake. But the tip of its nose is red, and the yellow rings on its body are bordered by black.

Most **garter snakes**, or **ribbon snakes**, have three stripes the full length of their bodies. These may be cream, yellow, or bright orange.

Ribbon snake

If a **hognosed snake** is come upon suddenly, it flattens its head, neck, and body and hisses loudly. It also strikes —but without opening its mouth.

If this does not frighten an enemy the snake rolls on its back and writhes. Then it lies still as though dead. But if it is turned onto its stomach, the hognosed snake quickly rolls onto its back again.

When all becomes quiet, the snake lifts its head and looks around. If it feels safe, it turns over and crawls away.

Hognosed snake

Snakes are popular as pets but often are mistreated.

Never keep snakes as pets to scare people. Never keep a poisonous snake as a pet.

Containers or cages must have light and air. But they must be very tight. Snakes can escape through even small openings.

In holding a snake, always hold its body in the middle. Never hold it only by its head or its tail.

If a snake will not eat, turn it loose. The best place to let it go is where you found it. If it does eat—and you can find out from books or a pet store about the right foods—a feeding every week in summer is enough. In winter, it may eat only once a month. Some snakes will eat hamburger. Others like only live food, such as mice or rats. Keep a small container of water in the cage, and give your snake a place to hide in or under.

Index

Anaconda, 29
Asp (Egyptian cobra), 31

Babies, snake, 21, 22
Black mambas, 18, 33
Boa constrictor, 29
Body temperature, 9
Bone structure, 25
Breathing, 9, 17
Bushmaster, 41

Cages, 47
Cleopatra, 31
Cobra, 27, 31-33
Constrictors, 13
Copperhead, 39
Coral snakes, 34
Cottonmouth (water
    moccasin), 39
Crawling, 10, 18-19

Eastern diamond-
    back, 38
Eating habits, 7, 12-17,
    44, 47
Eggs, snake, 20-22
"Egg tooth," 21
Egyptian cobra (asp), 31
Enemies of, 27
European viper, 6
Eyes, 10, 23

Fangs, 14, 40, 41

Fer-de-lance, 41

Gaboon viper, 41
Garter snake, common,
    22, 45

Hearing, 23
Hognosed snake, 46
Hogs, 26

Jaws, 16-17

Keel, 10
King cobra, 31
King snakes, 44-45

Legs, 29

Mambas, 18, 33
Mongoose, 27

People, 27
Pigmy rattlesnake, 38
Poison, 14, 31-32, 35
Pythons, 29

Racers, 43
Rat snakes, 43
Rattlesnakes, 38-40
Reptiles, 7-9
Reticulated python, 29
Ribbon snakes, 45
Russell's viper, 41

Scales, 10
Scarlet king snake, 45
Scarlet snake, 34
Sea snakes, 36-37
Secretary birds, 26
Seeing, 23
Shedding, 11, 39
"Sidewinders," 19
Snake charmer, 23
Snakes
    as pets, 47
    birth of, 20-22
    body temperature of, 9
    care of, 47
    eating habits of, 7, 12-17
        44, 47
    enemies of, 26-27
    poisonous, 14, 31-41
    relatives of, 7
    sea, 36-37
Speed, crawling, 18-19
Spitting cobra, 32
Swallowing, 15-17

Teeth, 15
Tongue, 24
Tuatara, 7

Vipers, 6, 40-41

Water moccasin
    (cottonmouth), 39
Weather, snakes and, 9